Dividing

PETER PATILLA

KINGFISHER
An imprint of Larousse plc
Elsley House
24-30 Great Titchfield Street
London W1P 7AD

First published in 1990 by Kingfisher
This edition published in 1997

10 9 8 7 6 5 4 3 2 1

A CIP catalogue record for this book is
available from the British Library.

ISBN 0 7534 0156 8

Editor: John Grisewood
Illustrations: Terry McKenna
Design: Robert Wheeler Design Associates

Phototypeset by Southern Positives and Negatives,
(SPAN), Lingfield, Surrey

Printed in Spain

Contents

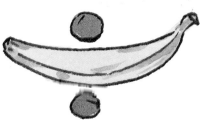
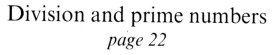

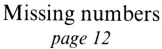
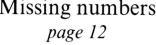

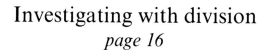

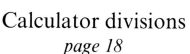

Division build up

There are lots of different ways of working out division problems.
Here are two ways.

Repeated subtraction

Division is a quick way of working out the answers to repeated
subtraction problems.

$12 \div 4$ *can mean:* how many times can you subtract four from 12?
or: how many fours in 12?

$12 - 4 - 4 - 4 = 0$ There are 3 fours in 12.

Try these repeated subtraction problems.

There are 27 segments in this giant orange.
How many children can have 3 segments each?

1 Drat = 100p

How many 20p coins are there in 1 Drat?
How many 5p coins are there in 1 Drat?

Start

$184.$

Finish

$100.$

How many 14's have been taken away?

4

Equal sharing

Division is also a way of sharing equally.

12 ÷ 4 can mean share 12 equally into four sets.

12 = ③ ③ ③ ③

The four sets will each contain 3.

Try these equal sharing problems.

There are 32 strawberries
in the box and there
are four children.
How many strawberries will
each child have?

Share 50p between two children. How much will each have?

Forty-eight shared into 3 sets.
Draw what would be in each set.

Division ways

There are lots of different ways of working out the answers to division problems.

Sometimes one method makes the division easier, other times another is easier.

Here are some different methods for you to explore.

You can use a calculator to check the answers.

Halving

$$6\overline{)516}$$

Not very good at dividing by 6?
Try halving both numbers.

$$3\overline{)258}$$

Now work out the answer.

Try halving both numbers on these problems.
Does it change the final answer?

$$6\overline{)312} \qquad 14\overline{)322} \qquad 18\overline{)828} \qquad 14\overline{)490}$$

Can you see how to change some long divisions into short division?

Sometimes you can halve and halve again.

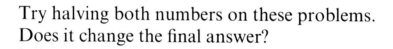

$12\overline{)672}$ halve $6\overline{)336}$ halve $3\overline{)168}$

Now try these.

$$8\overline{)472} \qquad 12\overline{)768} \qquad 16\overline{)464} \qquad 16\overline{)512}$$

Doubling

· 5)235

Dividing by 5 is not too hard but dividing by 10 is easier!
Try doubling both numbers.

10)470

Does the answer change?

Use the doubling method on these divisions.

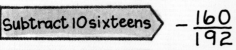

5)125   5)315   5)425   5)435

Subtracting

16)512

Let us find out how many sixteens there are in 512.
All you need to know is how to subtract and what 10 sixteens are.

$10 \times 16 = 160$

Subtract 10 sixteens	$-\begin{array}{r}512\\160\\\hline352\end{array}$	10
Subtract 10 sixteens	$-\begin{array}{r}160\\\hline192\end{array}$	10
Subtract 10 sixteens	$-\begin{array}{r}160\\\hline32\end{array}$	10
Subtract 1 sixteen	$-\begin{array}{r}16\\\hline16\end{array}$	1
Subtract 1 sixteen	$-\begin{array}{r}16\\\hline0\end{array}$	$\frac{1}{32}$

number of sixteens in 512

Try these. 14)574   16)656   23)529   26)806   21)1092

Remainders

Sometimes when we divide there is a remainder left over. Explore these division activities and learn more about remainders.

Remainders galore

Divide 2519 by each number from 1 to 10 in turn.
See what happens to the remainders.

$$\begin{array}{r} 2519\text{r}0 \\ 1)\overline{2519} \end{array} \qquad \begin{array}{r} 1259\text{r}1 \\ 2)\overline{2519} \end{array}$$

Now try 5039 divided by numbers from 1 to 10 in turn.

Zero remainders

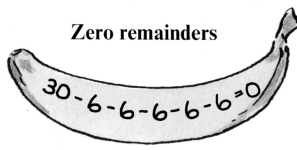

30 − 6 − 6 − 6 − 6 − 6 = 0

Start with 30.
Repeatedly subtract a single digit.
Which digits reach zero and have no remainder?

Try with different starting numbers.

Remainder puzzle

Divide each number by 8 to find the remainder.
Use the code to change remainders into letters.
Rearrange the letters to find the names of fruit.

CODE								
Remainder	0	1	2	3	4	5	6	7
Letter		B	N	O	A	R	G	E	P

28	22	35	23

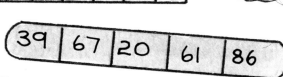

39	67	20	61	86

14	53	19	65	58	52

43	51	25	33	56	83

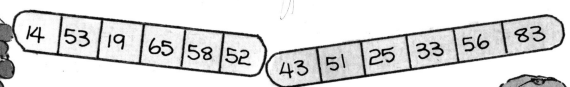

Remainder problem

Think of a number.
Divide it by 5
The remainder is 3.
What could the number have been?

The remainder is 4.
What could I have divided by?

Decimal remainders

Calculators do not give the remainders to division problems.
They turn the remainder into a decimal.

$$\begin{array}{r} 2r3 \\ 4\overline{)11} \end{array} \qquad \begin{array}{r} 2.75 \\ 4\overline{)11.00} \end{array}$$

Try to change these remainders into decimals.

$$\begin{array}{r} 11r1 \\ 2\overline{)23} \end{array} \qquad 2\overline{)23.0}$$

$$\begin{array}{r} 6r2 \\ 5\overline{)32} \end{array} \qquad \begin{array}{r} 6. \\ 5\overline{)32.0} \end{array}$$

$$\begin{array}{r} 4r2 \\ 4\overline{)18} \end{array} \qquad \begin{array}{r} 4. \\ 4\overline{)18.0} \end{array}$$

$$\begin{array}{r} 8r1 \\ 4\overline{)33} \end{array} \qquad \begin{array}{r} 8. \\ 4\overline{)33.00} \end{array}$$

Number search

I know a number which when
divided by 2, 3, and 5 does
not leave a remainder.
Can you discover my number?
Is there only one such number?

9

Division puzzles

Try these division puzzles. Knowing your tables will help!

Musical division

Work out each division fact. The answers tell you where to place the notes. Notes will be on a line or in a space.

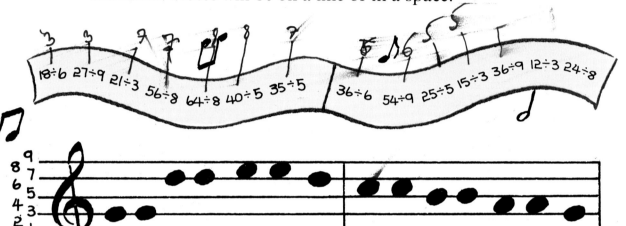

The tune is a nursery rhyme. What do you think it could be?

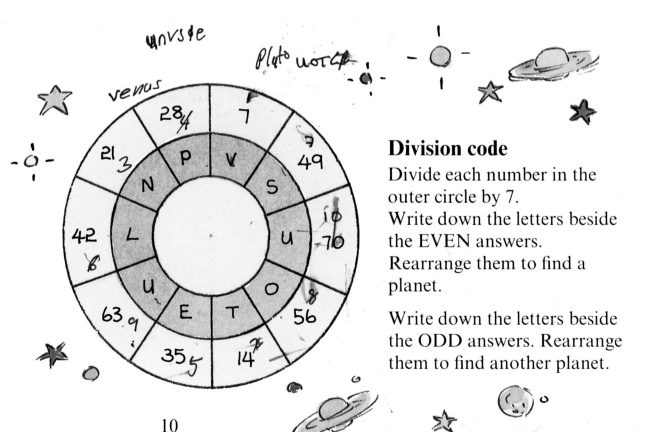

Division code

Divide each number in the outer circle by 7.
Write down the letters beside the EVEN answers. Rearrange them to find a planet.

Write down the letters beside the ODD answers. Rearrange them to find another planet.

Division maze

Get the wasp to the apple.
It can only pass numbers which are divisible by **6** or **9**.
How many routes can you find?

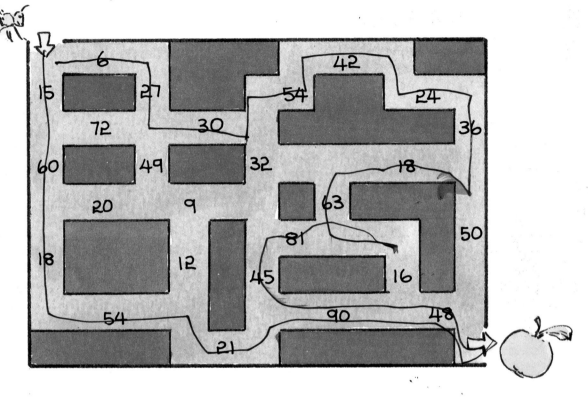

Division alphabet

Each letter of the alphabet has a number.

A	B	C	D	E	F	G	H	I	J	K	L	M	N	O	P	Q	R	S	T	U	V	W	X	Y	Z
1	2	3	4	5	6	7	8	9	10	11	12	13	14	15	16	17	18	19	20	21	22	23	24	25	26

Work out the answers to these division problems.
Find out the mystery words.

$$\frac{36}{9} \qquad \frac{90}{5} \qquad \frac{126}{6} \qquad \frac{52}{4}$$

$$\frac{72}{9} \qquad \frac{135}{9} \qquad \frac{54}{3} \qquad \frac{98}{7}$$

$$\frac{60}{3} \qquad \frac{72}{4} \qquad \frac{36}{4} \qquad \frac{10}{10} \qquad \frac{112}{8} \qquad \frac{49}{7} \qquad \frac{84}{7} \qquad \frac{25}{5}$$

What have the words in common?

Missing numbers in division

In these problems some numbers are missing. Sometimes there will be only one answer. Othertimes there will be several possible answers. Can you discover which is which?

Equations

$72 \div 9 = \boxed{8}$ $64 \div \boxed{8} = 8$ $\boxed{63} \div 7 = 9$

$54 \div \boxed{9} = 6$ $32 \div 8 = \boxed{4}$ $\boxed{42} \div 6 = 7$

Open equations

$24 \div \square = \triangle$ $\square \div \triangle = 3$ $36 \div \square = \triangle$

$\square \div \triangle = 5$ $21 \div \triangle = \square$ $\square \div \triangle = 8$

Missing digits

Each star is a missing digit.
Can you work out what it should be?

$$\begin{array}{r} 31 \\ *\overline{)124} \end{array} \qquad \begin{array}{r} 41 \\ 8\overline{)3{*}8} \end{array} \qquad \begin{array}{r} {*}9 \\ 5\overline{)4{*}5} \end{array} \qquad \begin{array}{r} 11{*} \\ {*}\overline{)702} \end{array}$$

Final digit

Each of these numbers is divisible by 9. The final digit of each number is missing. What should the digit be?

12

Function machines

Which numbers will leave the machine?

48 56 32 72 64 24

÷ 8

IN   OUT   ? ? ?

Which numbers were fed into the machine?

? ? ?   IN   ÷ 7   OUT   9 6 7 5 8 4

Table grids

Copy and complete these table grids.

×		7
4	36	
		42

×		8
		72
10	50	

×		
	12	24
	28	56

Chains

What are the missing numbers in this "halving" chain?

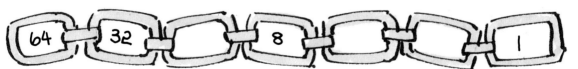

64   32   ☐   8   ☐   ☐   1

What are the missing numbers in this "quartering" chain?

4096   ☐   256   ☐   ☐   ☐   1

13

Division games

Use your division skills to play these games.

Fives and threes

Play dominoes in the usual way. As each domino is played total the numbers at each end. If the total is divisible by 5 or 3 the answer is the player's score. If the total is divisible by 5 AND 3 the score is the total of the two answers.

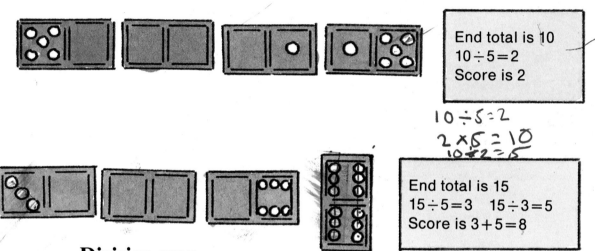

End total is 10
$10 \div 5 = 2$
Score is 2

$10 \div 5 = 2$
$2 \times 5 = 10$
$10 \div 2 = 5$

End total is 15
$15 \div 5 = 3$ $15 \div 3 = 5$
Score is $3 + 5 = 8$

Division snap

Use a deck of cards without the pictures.
Divide the cards between the players.

The game is played like SNAP except you total the cards as they are played.

When the total is divisible by 2 you call SNAP and those cards are yours.

You can change the rules so that SNAP is called when the total is divisible by 3.

14

Division star

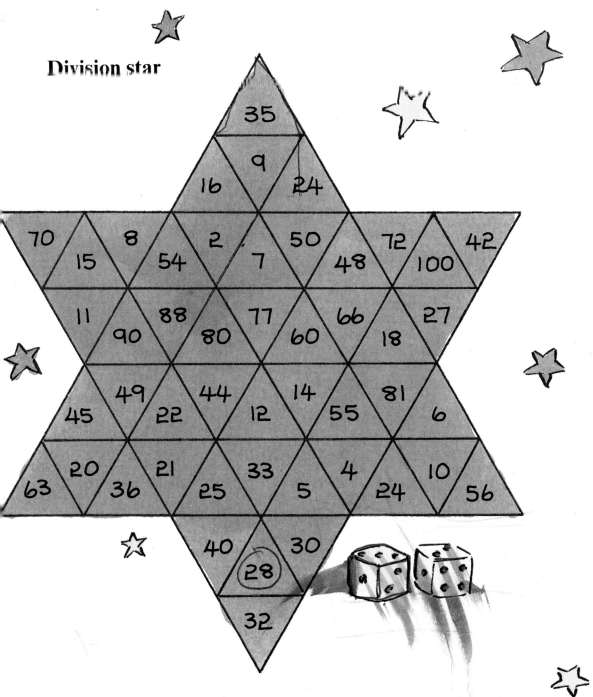

Roll 2 dice and total.

Cover any number on the star which this total will divide into exactly.

Game 1: First player to place 10 markers on the star wins.

Game 2: First player to have 4 touching markers wins.

Game 3: First player to complete a star point wins.

Game 4: The player who places most markers wins.

Investigating with division

Factor investigation

> 12 has six factors: : 1,2,3,4,6,12
> 17 has two factors : 1,17
> 9 has three factors : 1,3,9

Explore factors of numbers up to 50.

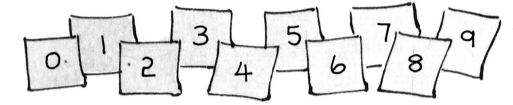

Which numbers have six factors?

Which numbers have only two factors?

Which numbers have an odd number of factors?

Digit card divisions

Use a set of digit cards numbered 0–9.

0 1 2 3 4 5 6 7 8 9

Use a division card. ÷

Make a set of four cards which give an exact answer.
No remainders allowed!
Here are two sets to start you off.

4 5 ÷ 9

3 4 ÷ 2

How many sets can you find?

Remainders

All these divisions give a remainder of 4.

$9 \div 5$	$25 \div 7$	$28 \div 8$	$54 \div 10$

Can you find other divisions which give a remainder of 4?
See if you can spot any patterns in your results.

Digit repeat

Here are the answers to some division problems.

$$6.6666666$$

$$2.2222222$$

$$11.111111$$

Which pairs of number could have been divided?
Find other parts of numbers which give answers of a repeating digit.

Forbidden key

You may use a calculator to answer these division problems . . . BUT . . . you must not touch the 5 key! Try to find different ways of doing each one.

$5\overline{)90}$ $9\overline{)135}$

$5\overline{)165}$ $4\overline{)252}$

NOT FIVE

17

Calculator divisions

A calculator can be used to help you divide large numbers. It can also be used to explore and experiment with division of numbers.

Double division

Enter a 3-digit number into your calculator.

$$536.$$

Make it a 6-digit number by repeating the same set of digits.

$$536536.$$

Divide by 7 . .

Divide this answer by 11 . .

Divide the answer by 13

What do you notice?

Try for other 6-digit numbers made in the same way.

Division estimator
An estimate is a "good guess" of the answer.
Choose the estimate you think is nearest the answer.

	ESTIMATES			ANSWERS
$873 \div 9$	0	50	100	
$525 \div 5$	100	150	200	
$1757 \div 7$	200	250	300	
$1448 \div 4$	300	350	400	
$1488 \div 3$	400	450	500	

Check your estimates by finding the answers.
Are you a good division estimator?

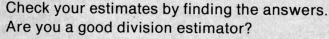

18

No remainders

You can only use these number keys.

You can only use these symbol keys.

Make up division problems which do not leave remainders, or give an answer with decimals.

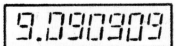   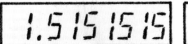

How many can you find?

Calculator quickies

Here is the answer to a division problem.

Can you make up ten division problems which give this answer?

Use your calculator to help you answer these problems.

$$\begin{array}{r} 437 \\ 6\overline{)****} \end{array} \qquad \begin{array}{r} 365 \\ **\overline{)4380} \end{array} \qquad \begin{array}{r} 156r* \\ 13\overline{)2037} \end{array}$$

Two-digit repeats

Start with 100 each time. Input one division operation.
Try to make these answers.

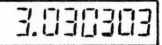 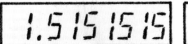 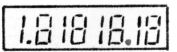

Factors and divisibility

Factors are whole numbers which will exactly divide into other whole numbers.
The factors of **12** are **1, 2, 3, 4, 6, 12**.
The factors of **15** are **1, 3, 5, 15**.

Factor trees

Here are some factor trees

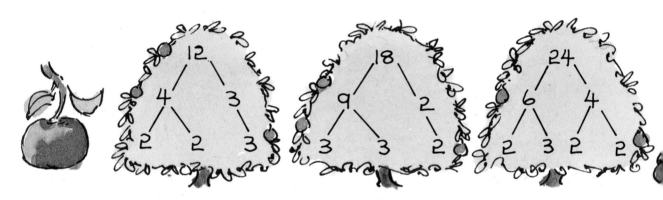

Can you see how each number is broken down into factors? If you multiply the numbers in each horizontal line you get the number you started with. Can you copy and complete these factor trees?

Factor query

Here are some factors of a number: 2   3   4
Which numbers, less than 50, could they be a factor of?

Divisible by 2

All even numbers are divisible by 2.
They have 2 as a factor.
Which of these numbers are divisible by 2?

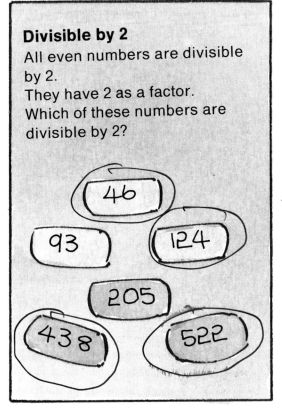

46
93
124
205
438
522

Divisible by 5 and 10

Numbers which end in 0 are divisible by 10 and 5.
Numbers which end in 5 are divisible by 5.
Which of these numbers are divisible by 5?

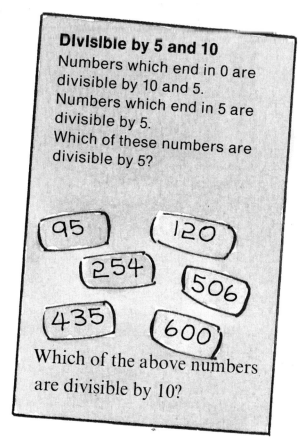

95
120
254
506
435
600

Which of the above numbers are divisible by 10?

Divisible by 4

Which of these numbers are divisible by 4?

236   120   314   211   332   516

Look carefully at the last two digits of the numbers.
Can you find a rule for testing whether a number is divisible by 4?

Leap Year dates are divisible by 4. Which of these events happened on a leap year?

1544 William Shakespeare Born

1066 Battle of Hastings

1953 Mount Everest Climbed

1840 Penny Post started

Division and prime numbers

Most whole numbers can be divided by another whole number without leaving a remainder.

A number which can only be divided by itself and one is called a PRIME NUMBER.

Explore these prime number activities.

Sieve of Eratosthenes

Eratosthenes was a Greek mathematician who lived 275–195 BC. He discovered the following method of finding prime numbers less than 100.

Copy this 100 grid.

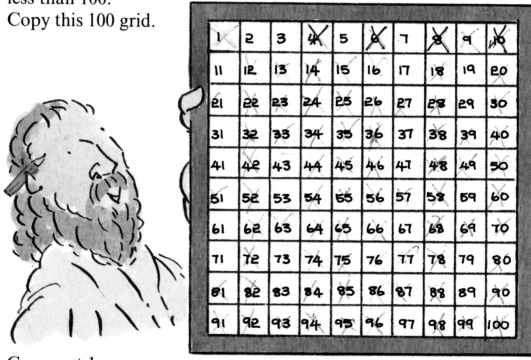

Cross out 1.

Cross out all numbers divisible by 2, but not 2.

Cross out all numbers divisible by 3, but not 3.

Cross out all numbers divisible by 5, but not 5.

Cross out all numbers divisible by 7, but not 7.

Make a list of the numbers not crossed out.

These are prime numbers.

Domino primes

Here is a domino square.
The total of spots on each side is
a prime number.
Can you make some prime
number domino squares?

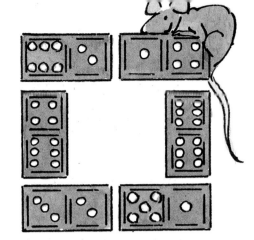

Card primes

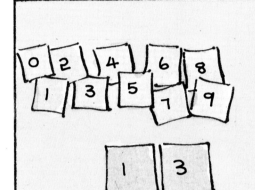

Use a set of digit cards 0–9.

Arrange the cards to make 1-digit
and 2-digit numbers.

 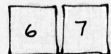

Each number must be a prime number.
Can you use up all the cards?

Prime quiz

True or false?

Add one or subtract one from any prime number greater than 3.
Six will always divide into the answer.

In any consecutive twelve numbers under 100 there will always be at
least two prime numbers.

There is always a prime number between consecutive square
numbers up to 100.

Division, decimals and fractions

Decimals and fractions keep on popping up when you are exploring and investigating division.

Decimal divisions

7)6.

A calculator turns a remainder into a decimal.

$25 \div 2 = 12.5$

Here are answers to five division problems. Find a pair of numbers which will divide to give each answer.

Which decimal remainders are possible if you divide by:

8   5   4   10

Repeating divisions

Some divisions do not work out exactly.
They go on, and on, and on . . .

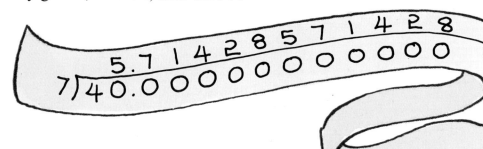

Which of these divisions go on, and on . . .

7)36   9)34   5)28   6)27   3)41   8)75

Can you discover which dividing numbers make divisions go on, and on . . .?

$$\frac{22}{24}$$

$$\frac{100}{200}$$

Dividing fractions

$\frac{3}{4}$ can mean $4\overline{)3.00}$ with 0.75 above

$\frac{2}{5}$ can mean $5\overline{)2.0}$ with 0.4 above

Can you change these fractions into decimals?

$$\frac{3}{8} \qquad \frac{4}{5} \qquad \frac{1}{2} \qquad \frac{7}{8} \qquad \frac{3}{10} \qquad \frac{1}{4}$$

Nearly fractions

Some fractions do not change into decimals exactly.

$\frac{2}{3} \Rightarrow 3\overline{)2.000000\ldots\ldots}$ with $0.666666\ldots\ldots$ above

Which of these fractions do not change into decimals exactly?

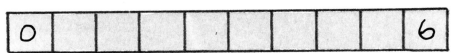

$$\frac{4}{7} \qquad \frac{5}{6} \qquad \frac{5}{8} \qquad \frac{7}{9} \qquad \frac{1}{3} \qquad \frac{2}{5}$$

Dice game

Each player needs a grid like this.

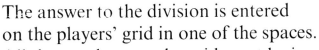

Players take turns to roll two
dice to show two numbers.
They decide in which order to
divide the two numbers.
The answer to the division is entered
on the players' grid in one of the spaces.
All the numbers on the grid must be in correct order.
Numbers cannot be entered twice.
Who can complete the grid first?

$3 \div 4 = 0.75$
or $4 \div 3 = 1.3333$

Measuring and division

Division skills can be used when we are measuring.

Length problem

Wall paper is usually sold in rolls which are 10 metres long. Measure the height of your room. How many lengths would you get from one roll?

Paper thickness

How thick do you think a sheet of paper is?
Measure a thick book.
Check the numbers of pages.
Can you calculate the thickness of one page?

Light weight

Can you find out how heavy one dried pea is?
Start by weighing lots of dried peas!
Try finding the weight of some other light objects.

Best buys
Which of these are the best buys?

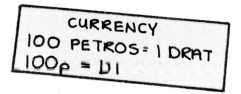

CEREAL
D1.20
750g

CEREAL
D1.50
1kg

D2.40
750ml

D3.50
1 LITRE

D1.50

D1.95

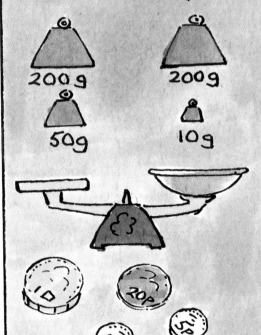

Part measures
Total each set.   Find $\frac{1}{4}$ of each.

200g   200g

50g   10g

Liquid measures
A medicine spoon holds 5ml.
How many doses will there be
in each medicine bottle?

COUGH
400ml

SNEEZE
550ml

STOMACH
750ml

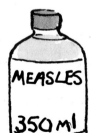

MEASLES
350ml

27

Division data handling

One way of showing
information is with a pie chart.

This is a pie chart divided into
the 24 hours of a day.

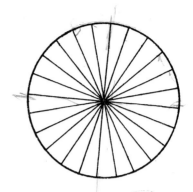

Here are pie charts showing how
four children spent one Tuesday.

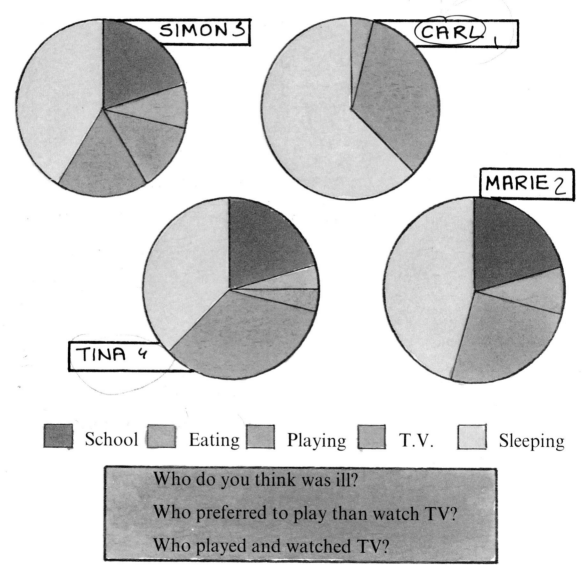

SIMON 3   CARL 1

MARIE 2

TINA 4

School   Eating   Playing   T.V.   Sleeping

Who do you think was ill?

Who preferred to play than watch TV?

Who played and watched TV?

Make a pie chart to show how you spend a day

Glossary

Consecutive numbers: These are numbers which follow on from each other e.g 10, 11, 12 and 56, 57, 58, 59

Digits: The digits are: 0, 1, 2, 3, 4, 5, 6, 7, 8, 9
Some numbers have two digits (35, 78, 95)
Some numbers have three digits (108, 567, 856)

Estimation: An estimation is a sensible guess

Even Numbers: Numbers which can be divided exactly by two.
Here are some even numbers: 2, 6, 18, 74, 90, 142

Factors: Factors are whole numbers which will exactly divide into other whole numbers.
The factors of 8 are 1, 2, 4, 8
The factors of 20 are 1, 2, 4, 5, 10, 20

Multiples: The multiples of 2 are 2 4 6 8 10 12 . . .
The multiples of 3 are 3 6 9 12 15 18 . . .
The multiples of 4 are 4 8 12 16 20 24 . . .

Odd Numbers: Numbers which cannot be divided by two without leaving a remainder.
Here are some odd numbers: 3, 5, 27, 41, 89, 125

Prime Numbers: Prime numbes can only be divided by themselves and one. The prime numbers less than 100 are:
1 2 3 5 7 11 13 17 19 23 29 31 37 41 43 47 53 59 61 67 71 73 79 83 89 97

Square Numbers: A square number is obtained by multiplying a number by itself.
36 is a square number because $6 \times 6 = 36$
81 is a square number because $9 \times 9 = 81$

Total: To total a set of numbers means to add them together. The total of 12, 20 and 34 is 66.

Answers

Page 4:
Repeated subtraction
9 children; 5 coins, 20 coins; 6

Page 5:
Equal sharing
8 strawberries; 25p;
16 in each set.

Page 6:
Halving
52; 23; 46; 35
59; 64; 29; 32

Page 7:
Doubling
25; 63; 85; 87

Subtracting
41; 41; 23; 31; 52

Page 8:
Remainders galore
The remainders are 0, 1, 2, 3, 4, 5, 6, 7, 8, 9

Zero remainders
1, 2, 3, 5, 6

Remainder Puzzle
Pear, grape, orange, banana

Page 9:
Remainder Problem
Any number greater than 4;
8, 13, 18, etc

Decimal Remainders
11.5; 6.4; 4.5; 8.25

Number Search
60, 90, 120, etc

Page 10:
Musical Division
Twinkle, Twinkle Little Star

Division Code
Pluto; Venus

Page 11:
Division Maze
There are 2 routes

Division Alphabet
Drum, Horn, Triangle (All musical instruments)

Page 12:
Equations
8; 8; 63; 9; 4; 42

Open Equations

1,24	3,1	1,36	5,1	1,21	8,1
2,12	6,2	2,18	10,2	3,7	16,2
3,8	9,3	3,12	15,3	7,3	24,3
4,6	12,4	4,9	20,4	21,1	32,4
6,4	15,5	6,6	25,5		40,5
8,3	etc	9,4	etc		etc
12,2		12,3			
24,1		18,2			
		36,1			

Missing Digits
4; 2; 8,4; 6,7

Final Digit
432, 747, 306, 846, 954

Page 13:
Function machines
Out: 3, 8, 9, 4, 7, 6
In: 63, 42, 49, 35, 56, 28

Table Grids (a possible answer)

×	9	7
4	36	28
6	54	42

×	5	8
9	45	72
10	50	80

×	4	8
3	12	24
7	28	56

Chains
64, 32, 16, 8, 4, 2, 1
4096, 1024, 256, 64, 16, 4, 1

Page 18:
Division Estimator
100; 100; 250; 350; 500

Page 19:
Calculator Quickies
2622; 12; r9

Two-digit Repeats
11; 66; 55; 33; 22; 99

Page 20:
Factor Trees

36		48		32	
4	9	6	8	4	8
2 2	3 3	3 2 2 4		2 2 4 2	
		3 2 2 2 2		2 2 2 2 2	

Factor Query
12, 24, 36, 48

Page 21:
Divisible by 2
46, 124, 438, 522

Divisible by 5
95, 120, 435, 600

Divisible by 10
120, 600

Divisible by 4
236, 120, 332, 516
1544, 1840

Page 22:
Sieve of Eratosthenes
The prime numbers are:
1 2 3 5 7 11 13 17 19 23 29 31 37 41 43
47 53 59 61 67 71 73 79 83 89 97

Page 23:
Prime Quiz
True, true, true

Page 24
Decimal Divisions
Possible dividing numbers include:
1 and 4, 1 and 8, 5 and 8,
3 and 4, 2 and 5.
.2, .4, .6, .8
.25, .5, .75
.1, .2, .3, .4, .5, .6, .7, .8, .9
There are several possible answers to
each problem.

Repeating Divisions
Dividing by 7, 9, 3 produces repeating
decimals.
Dividing by 6 sometimes produces
repeating decimals.

Page 25
Dividing Fractions
0.375: 0.8: 0.5: 0.875: 0.3: 0.25 5

Nearly Fractions
4/7: 5/6: 7/9: 1/3 3

Page 27
Best Buys
D1.50: D2.40: D1.95 2

Part Measures
115g. 10p. 1

Liquid Measures
80; 110; 150; 70 3

Page 28
Carl; Marie; Simon and Tina 2 1 2nd

Index